UNSTUCK

DISCOVERING

CAREER

LIMITING

ACTIONS

UNSTUCK

DISCOVERING

CAREER

LIMITING

ACTIONS

Dethra U. Giles, MBA,MSCM, SPHR

"Unstuck Discovering Career Limitng Actions" Copyright © 2014 by Detra U. Giles

ISBN: 13: 978-1-934947-82-1

First Asta Publications, LLC trade paperback edition

Printed in the United States of America

DEDICATION

Thank you to my dear husband, Frank L. Giles, who has supported this vision and always believed in me, even when I had doubts; to my beautiful babies, Jairah and Daniel Giles, who are respectively my favorite daughter and favorite son; and to my Dream Catcher, Margaret "Terri" Daniels, my mom, for sacrificing herself so I could be someone no one ever expected me to be.

Table of Contents

Only those who will risk going too far can possibly find out how far one can go. ~T.S. Eliot

If hard work were such a wonderful thing, surely the rich would have kept it all to themselves. ~Lane Kirkland

Sometimes the path you're on is not as important as the direction you're heading. ~Kevin Smith

Your work is going to fill a large part of your life, and the only way to be truly satisfied is to do what you believe is truly great work. And the only way to do great work is to love what you do. If you haven't found it yet, keep looking, and don't settle. As with all matters of the heart, you'll know when you find it. ~Steve Jobs

The question isn't who is going to let me; it's who is going to stop me. ~Ayn Rand

There is one quality more important than "know-how." This is "know-what" by which we determine not only how to accomplish our purposes, but what our purposes are to be. ~Norbert Wiener

The shortest distance between two points assumes you know where you're going. ~Robert Brault

Chapter 7..**30**
If you are irreplaceable you are unpromotable. ~Dethra U. Giles

Introduction

Only those who will risk going too far can possibly find out how far one can go.
~T.S. Eliot

A Check:

Years ago I began my career in academia. My first position in the academy was as an Employee Relations Specialist in the Human Resources division of a large, southern university, located in Atlanta, Georgia. My first boss there was a woman by the name of Sonya Richburg, she was a brilliant woman who taught me a great deal. Shortly into my tenure at the university, Sonya taught me a lesson that has stayed with me as a professional and I use it to this very day.

While new in my role at the university I identified a problem I felt should be solved. After presenting the problem to my boss, who agreed the problem needed to be resolved, I was tasked with presenting the problem and ideas for solutions to a committee of decision makers. I worked hard to prepare for a meeting where I was going to present my ideas on the topic. I thought the ideas were great ideas because they were well researched, looked at all sides of the issues and considered the resources needed and available to solve the problem. The University needed a solution to the problem. I prepared, worked hard, researched and had sound facts and data to support the project and the direction I was recommending. Everyone listened, they liked the ideas and even complimented me on doing a great job with the presentation, right before they said "No" to all of my ideas. The project was given a red light and would not go forward.

Not only did they say "No" to my ideas, they also said "Yes" to the continued existence of the problem. I was upset and felt like a failure. I went back to my office and sulked. Sonya, in her infinite wisdom, walked into my office, put a sticky note on the computer screen in front of me and walked away. I studied the yellow sticky note and the red check mark she had placed on it. I looked at it confused and said "Wait a minute. Are you going to put this on my screen and walk away? What is this?" She looked at me, chuckled and said "Honey, this is your reality check. First of all, working here is like working in dog years, each one is actually like seven. Secondly, just because you have a good idea and a good presentation does not mean it is a good time. Your idea could flop for several reason it does not mean you sulk or stop producing ideas, it just means that idea didn't fly. Get over it. Lastly, and most importantly, there is actually a possibility, though you think it slight, that you could be wrong." Sonya, was a great boss, actually, one of the best bosses I ever had.

Today those words make me laugh when I think about them but I still find them to be profound. It was a reality check I needed and am glad Sonya gave.

Today I find that many professionals have never had a Sonya Richburg, that person, somewhere in their career who gave them a much needed reality check. Because they have never had a reality check they are struggling and confused about why they are in their current predicament and/or how to get out. The purpose of this book is to help with that. This book is your yellow sticky note with a red check in the middle, stuck to your computer screen, looking at you as you are looking at it. This is your reality check.

Following Instructions:

Go to school, get a good job, do a good job and stay out of trouble. Those words told to me by my grandmother echoed in my ears for years. I brought the plan hook line and sinker. I wanted to be the head of someone's company, that was my success aspiration. Based on what my grandmother told me, I believed, if I went to school I would excel in the professional world, so I went to school and acquired three college degrees- it didn't work. I thought if I got a good job, with good benefits, I would get to the top of the organization, but again, no luck. I thought if I did a good job I would get that corner office, so, I came to work before everyone else, left later than everyone else, took on more projects and worked myself into burnout, still, my results were nothing compared to what I was putting in. Sure, I would get the annual increases just like everyone else and even got a nice, expensive plaque with accolades about my hard work engraved on it. But, I was not moving. Not like Bob, who started with me but ended up being my boss or Sam who came in after me, was trained by me and ended up being Bob's boss.

It's Not Me, it's Them

There was Bob, Sam, John, Josh and even a Robert. One thing they all had in common was they got promoted and I did not. There had to be a reason and I was not it. Or, was I? I had no desire to look within or to explore any rational reasons other than the obvious. Aside from the commonality of being promoted when I was not, Bob, Sam, John, Josh and Robert were all white males. Eureka, that's it. No problem with me, I was at a company that clearly had discriminatory practices. Instead of looking deeply, I looked at the surface reason and did the misinformed math: white guys, started after me, were trained by me, getting promoted ahead of me equals intentional discrimination of some sort, right? Right, until Shaun, a young black female, came in, was trained by me and also surpassed me. Shaun was followed by Roderick, who eventually passed us all. I must pause here to make a very important statement: discrimination is very real, alive and well with legitimate victims to prove it. I will not make light of the fact that discrimination exists but I will say that discrimination is like the devil; it gets a lot more credit than it deserves for things it is not actually responsible for doing. Discrimination has very real victims but, in these instances, I was not one of them. I was no victim of discrimination, I was a victim of a flawed way of professional existence. So flawed that I was strategically taking actions that would limit my career with the thought that I was advancing myself. I was stuck and did not know it, nor did I know how to get "Unstuck."

The Gift

Shaun and Roderick, not their real names, were gifts; they made me have to eliminate the perceived reasons for my situation and explore other options. Not only was Shaun an African American female, like me, she was also close to my age, had a similar level of experience but she was not in my situation; Shaun was climbing the ladder three rungs at a time. He, Roderick, was very similar to Shaun, only he was a male, and he was taking the company over one position at a time, at a rapid pace. I had to look for another answer to my plight. I had to acknowledge that I was doing something wrong, or not doing something that I should in order to make my career move. I had to accept the possibility that I was taking action, making moves that limited my career.

Solution Explorations

Once I acknowledged and accepted that my situation was likely not the result of discrimination I had to make a choice: either I was going to lie down and die, stuck in perpetual middle management or I was going to fight my way lose from the career limiting actions, get "unstuck" and then get to the top.

Die or Fight

As I identified my two options the image of the LaBrea Tar Pits of Los Angeles came to mind. I envisioned a prehistoric mammoth in the tar pit, fighting to get out, not realizing that the very thing he was doing in an attempt to save his life was getting him more stuck and closer to death. Thousands of years later people would marvel at his bones and talk about how massive, powerful, beautiful and great he was. They would speak of his lineage and the other animals that came from him while looking at the bones of the dead animal who got stuck and never made it; the animal who died right where he was. Then, I thought about the animals who got out of the tar pit. While they were few and far between, there were those that did escape. They got out of the tar pit. How? I don't really know how the other animals got out, but they did. Though the research is not expressly clear on how, I can tell you they did something different than the other animals that got stuck, stayed stuck, sunk deeper into their "stuckness" and died. I am sure those stuck animals that watch their counterparts escape thought like I did. I am sure the mammoth looked at the squirrel and thought, "Of course she can get unstuck; she is two pounds and I am tons." The mammoth likely made this excuse while not taking the opportunity to look around and see other squirrels dying too and not observing that the squirrel who did break free had a different technique from everyone else who was stuck and sinking to their death. It was her technique that made the squirrel successful, not the weight or lack there of.

The Decision to Fight

I am a fighter; laying down to die while there is still the ability to fight left in my body is something I just cannot imagine. In my exploration I wanted to understand how to fight better, as a result, I continued my inquiry. During my time of solution exploration I found some very interesting things. One of the most profound things I found was that I was not alone, actually, I, for once, was in the majority. Like in the tar pits, most of the professionals around me were not escaping, they remained stuck. The Bobs, Sams, Shauns and Rodericks were the minority; most people were working hard, not getting very far and, like me, were stuck. Many had given up on achieving career success, some refused to give up but had no clue about what to do differently and others had turned the corner from being "one of the best employees this company has ever seen," to "I don't know why they still have a job." Being the "HR Lady" I was privy to all this information. I would have supervisor after supervisor come into my office bewildered and say "I don't know what happened. They use to be my best..." In an effort to help supervisors manage the performance of the once great employee, I would look at old performance evaluations. The evaluations would be stellar; exceeds expectations ratings across the board, with statements like, "We could not survive without this employee", "They saved the company over a million dollars on this project", and the one that stood out to me the most was, "He will run this company one day." To have the same manager who wrote "He will run the company one day" sit in my office and ask me how to terminate the employment of a person he wrote this glowing phrase about, made me realize I had to do something. Though this was an extreme case, this was happening all over the company and in other companies. People who came in guns blazing, kicking butt and taking names had lost their luster and reconciled themselves to mediocrity: come to work, do their job, just enough to not get fired, go home to start it all over again tomorrow with a reward of the menial 2% annual increase and maybe a small promotion which is more of a title change than an actual promotion.

My Vow

Once I concluded my solution exploration I realized the problem I was experiencing was not unique to me. Actually, a great deal of the workforce found themselves in similar situations and were having the same emotions I was having. They were stuck and did not know they were stuck, did not know how they got stuck and did not know how to get unstuck. As I furthered my exploration I found this phenomena was not unique to employees: I began to find this phenomena with managers and teams, leaders and organization, business owners and the growth of their business: being stuck was an epidemic and like a medical epidemic it was deadly. Once my eyes opened to this phenomena I made a vow: I vowed to figure this thing out, get unstuck and then go back to get others unstuck as well. With this vow I became a mad scientist.

How I Got my Tick

If you know any mad scientist- after years in the academy I know a few- they often have a twitch, a little tick they were not born with. They got this tick from violating the rules of research. Many scientist take on research for personal reasons, either they themselves, someone close to them or a community they have an affinity for has been plagued with a particular disease and they have vowed to find a cure, even if it kills them. Mad scientist will often try the experiments on themselves. They give themselves a disease or they are already plagued with the disease and then they try to cure the disease with what they have discovered in their research. It is often a test before the real test or clinical trials to see if the cure works. Sometimes it does and sometimes it doesn't. Sometimes the test causes a little harm and sometimes it causes death. For the most part they don't die but the result is a small tick, a small price to pay for finding a groundbreaking cure. Well, that's me, I am the mad scientist who has tried the experiments on herself to see if they work. Some worked, some didn't, but, I am still alive and still experimenting. My research has not killed me yet but my story is still being written.

Clinical Trials

After trying the experiments on myself and having successful results, I decided the time had come for clinical trials. I found groups of people who were so frustrated with their situation that they agreed to be party to my experimentation. The trials had positive results-even better results than I had expected. I fully expected for people to improve in their career, but, I did not expect people to come back to me and say their marriage had been saved or that they had become a better parent. I think the response that floored me the most was the person who said "I am quitting my job and I don't have one to go to." They said this with a smile and a radiant glow. I realized I was on to something. This "stuck" thing was bigger than career, job, work. Being stuck at work permeated its way into peoples' state of being, their entire life. I realized if I helped people get unstuck professionally, I could help them change their lives inside and outside of the office.

Safe for the Market

Career advice, like any product, must have a clinical trial with documented results and those results must be evaluated before anyone agrees that the product is safe for the public to use. The results of my clinical trial proved, to me, that my process was not only safe but necessary and needed by the masses. There is an overwhelming number of people stuck in their career with no clue how to get free. This state of being stuck is doing more than frustrating them at work, it is causing medical issues, personal issues, home issues and the list goes on. Today, the company I founded, ExecuPrep, has helped hundreds of people rethink how they do this thing we call work. Through conferences, work with organizations, companies, industry leaders and individuals, ExecuPrep has given people the tools to challenge the traditional rules of career advancement and has given them the tools to get unstuck.

Chapter One

If hard work were such a wonderful thing, surely the rich would have kept it all to themselves.
~Lane Kirkland

Executive Summary

Jane has been working at Company X for 15 years. She is excellent at her job, one of the best. She consistently gets "exceptional" ratings on her performance evaluation, she is selected for all the top projects and she is the go to person for information. The problem is Jane has been in the same position for the last seven (7) years. Yes, Jane has been in the black whole of "Middle Management." Jane rationalized her situation and convinced herself, and others to whom she confides, that her "Middle Management" situation is the fault of the proverbial "glass ceiling".

Why is Jane not advancing? Why are you not advancing? The answer to both questions are likely the same. Discrimination, the glass ceiling, institutional racism are very real things, and they get way more credit than they deserve. According to the EEOC (Equal Employment Opportunity Commission), the federal agency charged with enforcing federal laws that make it illegal to discriminate against a job applicant or an employee because of the person's race, color, religion, sex (including pregnancy), national origin, age (40 or older), disability or genetic information, over 70% of discrimination cases have a "no cause" finding. This means, after a complaint is filed, an investigation is conducted and the investigation results show that the adverse action was not as a result of discrimination. Does this mean the adverse action did not happen, that a person did not get the promotion they deserved? No, it means they probably did not get the promotion they deserve, but, it was not because they were a woman, disabled, minority, over 40, or any of the other protected categories. In the absence of knowledge and information, people make up things. Jane and many people in Jane's situation cannot identify the reason they were over looked, once again, for a promotion that was rightfully theirs and likely given to a person they trained. While hitting the glass ceiling is a very real phenomenon it is not the reason why Jane and many other middle managers are stuck in the middle.

Then why?

There is rarely one, definitive reason why a person is not moving upward or is stuck in their career. There is typically a series of actions, events and /or circumstances that resulted in the stuck situation. These things are typically able to be categorized into two areas:

1. They do not know how they got to the middle; and
2. They do not know where they are going

Let's demystify the path from the middle to the Executive Suite and beyond. This will come first by identifying the "top" followed by identifying the best route for the individual to get there.

Chapter Two

Sometimes the path you're on is not as important as the direction you're heading.
~Kevin Smith

How did I get here?

The sad truth is that many people who have achieved "success," are not able to articulate how they got to their current position. Many of these people are unable to effectively coach or mentor others because they don't understand and are unable to clearly communicate how they have achieved their own level of success. When asked "how did you do it?" Their only response is "I did my job." Why is this a problem? There is a saying that goes "A people who do not know their history are doomed to repeat it." This saying is typically in reference to groups who have come out of horrid situations like the Holocaust, slavery or attempted genocide. The idea is that if the youth of these people forget what their ancestors endured, they, the youth, will not be watchful and mindful of the symptoms and signs that such events are on the verge of happening again. It is rare that you hear this quote in relation to success, but, the same is true. People who have been successful but do not know their history, i.e. the path they took to their current position are doomed to be unable to repeat the same steps and get the same results. These professionals find themselves making lateral moves for more money with no substantial improvement in position, power or authority. Knowing how you got to your present point means you clearly understand the tools and techniques that made you "successful." It also means you understand the tools well enough to make adjustments in their usage.

Tool Usage

A common mistake made by professionals is thinking "How I got here will be the same way I get there." Let's dispel that myth now. Before we had GPS navigation readily available, people had to get and give explicit directions. When a person visited a new place or went to someones home, they had to write down turn by turn directions. The person interpreting the directions was responsible for clearly writing the directions and then following the directions. They would often get to their destination, have a wonderful event and prepare to leave. It was a rare instance for a person to ask for directions back to their original location. Why wouldn't someone ask for directions back to their original location? Because, they would assume they could travel the same path: thinking the path that got them to their current destination should also be able to get them to their next destination. Many drivers have had that sinking feeling of realizing their assumption was wrong; the path that got them to one destination was an inadequate path to get them to another destination. However, drivers that were familiar with the area, even if not familiar with the current location, typically did not have the same issues. They understood the path they took and could easily identify parallel streets, alternate highway entrances and the like. They understood the path they used could be a guide, but, how they traveled the path needed adjusting if they were to make it to their intended destination. It was because they understood the path they traveled that they were better able to navigate to their next destination with ease.

The above analogy rings true for a career. Understanding how career success was achieved is important. This understanding allows you to repeat the steps your took for initial success, but also, so you are able to properly adjust and alter your new path to a new destination. Understand that it is not the duplication of the "same" tools that you need to achieve the next level in your career, but instead, the modified duplication of those tools. Think of your career as a building with every job you could ever have inside the building: each floor represents a higher level in your career with the top floors being the Ivory Tower, the Executive/Officer Suite. Understanding the path to success and how to alter it is the difference between having the keys to the fourth floor where you are able to move around freely but only make lateral moves on the fourth floor and having the master key to the entire building, including the highly coveted top floor.

Epic Fails

Knowing a history is not just about the tools that allowed success, it is also about the failures that allowed for valuable lessons. Success, if put into a Mathematical equation, would be, success= ((opportunity + preparation) timing + what to do)/what not to do. Knowing what not to do is a game changer, it is often more important than knowing what to do. Failures are indeed a key to success and often the thing most people overlook when identifying their path to their current position. Professionals will often note those things they did right and well, like going to college. But, they will often not take the time to reflect on things they did poorly or wrong, like picking the wrong major or accepting a job with the wrong company.

What has been your key failures? Key failures are those failures that were instrumental in your learning process; they are failures that needed to happen because without them you would not have gained the information you needed to move forward. Identifying these failures is often the hardest part.

Most people do not want to reflect on failures, successes, let's talk about those all day, but,many brush over their failures. Professionals speak of their failures as if they were minor pebbles in their path on the way to success instead of truthfully speaking of them as the self-imposed forks in the road or the road blocks that they actually were and are. For many professionals, their failures were career altering events, the failure(s) completely changed the trajectory of their career, many times for the better. The change happened not because the outcome of the failure was so great but because the lesson of "what not to do" was so profound. Growing up my mother would say "I can't tell you what my child won't do but, I can tell you what she won't do again." Knowing what to not do again was instrumental to my survival. The same is true for your career. Professionals must learn to value the lessons of their failures and consider those failures just as integral to the career achievements as their successes.

The path to where you are professionally is a culmination of right paths, wrong turns, u-turns and do-overs. Acknowledging the importance of each and understanding the role(s) they played in your success is very important when making your strategic plan to achieve your ultimate career goal.

Chapter Three

Your work is going to fill a large part of your life, and the only way to be truly satisfied is to do what you believe is truly great work. And the only way to do great work is to love what you do. If you haven't found it yet, keep looking, and don't settle. As with all matters of the heart, you'll know when you find it.
~Steve Jobs

What do I want to be when I grow up?

Human interaction is an interesting thing. It is intriguing to watch and listen to the questions complete strangers will ask one another, with the expectation of a clear, concise and reasonable answer. This is even more interesting when it comes to adult to child interaction. When meeting a new child the typical adult will ask the child "So, what do you want to be when you grow up?" Have you ever wondered why adults always ask little children, ages five and six, this question? Think about it for just a second, why would a child, so young, have a clue what they want to spend the rest of their lives doing as a source of income, a career, a profession? The truth; many of these adults, who should know "what they want to be when they grow up", are selfishly asking because they are looking for ideas.

There is one vital key to any and every successful journey: the destination. It does not matter how fancy the mode of transportation that may be fully equipped with the latest technology and navigation system, if an individual, item, product, etc. is going to successfully reach a desired destination, that destination must be set and communicated. A career goal is no different. A professional can have any number of degrees, certifications, designation, years of experience, written articles...but none of that matters if they do not have a final destination. One of the vital keys to movement in a career is the determination of where that career is going. Knowing where your career is going is the difference between deciding to swim from Miami to Cuba or just treading water in the Ocean: one is a challenging task but doable if you want to put in the work required and the other will provide a workout but will produce very little results in advancing your travel situation.

This lack of direction is the nemesis to getting unstuck. There are several things that get professionals stuck in their career, but, not knowing their personals career goal is the super glue of career limiting actions. I am always reminded of an interaction in the book "Alice's Adventures in Wonderland" or the movie, very closely titled "Alice in Wonderland" where Alice asks the Cheshire cat for directions and he responds by asking her where she is trying to go. She replied that she did not know where she going, to which the Cheshire Cat replied "well, any path will do." Following that scene, Alice spends the rest of the novel "finding" her way. Many professionals are like Alice: they have no clue where they are going and thusly any path will, frustratingly, suffice. They are traveling any path hoping to find what they are looking for on their journey and like Alice, they will find a host of character, interesting experiences and disturbing actions by themselves and others, all the while hoping to stumble upon a career that is desirable. Hope is a wonderful thing to have, a great thing to encourage in others, a needed piece of the human experience and a phenomenal campaign slogan, but, hope is not a strategy and especially, not a good career strategy. Teachers hope students will read their text books but they provide as syllabus with a plan for learning, police officers hope people won't drive too fast but they systematically park in locations where they can be seen and periodically pull people over so others are clear that the speed limits will be enforced, parents hope their children will abide by the house rules but they have a system of rewards and consequences for behavior outside of what has been deemed acceptable for their household. What if each of these people, teachers, police officers and parents, only used their hope to get their intended goals accomplished? It is not a far jump to conclude society would be over populated by a bunch of uneducated, fast driving, undisciplined people. Hope is not a strategy. The journey should be taken with the end in mind, not with the hope that the path will somehow reveal a magical, un-thought out, not planned for, pleasing destination. In most instances, the destination will not reveal itself but instead will be very elusive until the professional makes a decision.

The career goal must also have a certain level of clarity: the professional should be able to communicate it clearly to others who ask or who may be able to help. "I want to be a CEO" is not clear. Any individual is able to be a CEO at any given moment. If one wants to officially be the CEO of a "legitimate" company, it simply requires filing out paperwork with the

Secretary of State, stating on the paperwork that Ms...
is the CEO and voila, just like that, CEO. However, the
path to being the CEO of a Fortune 500 company may
not be such an easy task. Clarity matters: it determines
the strategy needed to reach the desired goal.

Clarity is also important when communicating with
those who are able to help with career goal achievement. No one makes it to their final destination alone:
helpers, mentors, advocates, cheerleaders are a must
have. These people can only be as effective as the professional is clear. These people are a part of the professionals career Navigation System, which means, they
can effectively guide when they have a clear destination that has been communicated. The role of mentors
will be discussed a little later but it is important to note
that the most effective mentoring relationship begins
with communication, by the mentee, of the intended
career destination.

Chapter Four

The question isn't who is going to let me; it's who is going to stop me.
~Ayn Rand

How do I get out?

"I am stuck." Say those words "I am stuck." Getting unstuck is like losing weight: people want a quick fix, to be in bathing suit shape by June but start the weight loss process in March. Just as people do not get out of shape over night, they also do not get stuck in their careers over night. Just as it took time and steps to get stuck, it will also take time and steps to get unstuck.

The first step to solving a problem is admitting the problem exists. A number of professionals do not recognize that they are, indeed, stuck. They have become so comfortable in their position that they don't realize they are getting a new set of peers every year because their peers are moving on and up while they remain in the same position year after year. Every position has a shelf life, the length of time a person should remain in that position; staying beyond the shelf life indicates the professional is indeed stuck.

The good news: the power to get unstuck is well within the reach of each professional who desires to get unstuck. The key word in the previous sentence is "desire." The person has to have a personal desire to change their situation. With this desire comes personal responsibility.

The second step to getting unstuck is taking responsibility.

No matter what anyone has done to you, or the impact it has had, you must take responsibility for achieving your own career goals. One of the biggest misconceptions employees have is that it is the job of the supervisor to advance the career of their subordinates. This could not be further from the truth. A supervisor's job is to develop subordinates to do their jobs well, to be a top performer and to even be the best at the tasks they perform; all of these may lead to career advancement for the subordinate but that is not the goal. The goal of a superior is to get the task(s) assigned to them done efficiently, effectively and well. The responsibility of career advancement belongs to the individual professional. Waiting in frustration for a supervisor to advance your career is not only career limiting it is also a poor use of good time. Moving your career is your responsibility, the sooner you accept that responsibility the sooner you will become unstuck.

The third step to getting unstuck is to look for the "why." There was a detective from the 70's that was good at looking for the "why." His name was Columbo, played by Peter Falk. Columbo was often viewed as the "stupid" detective because he spent his time asking, perceivably, dumb questions. But, those dumb questions routinely led him to solving the crime that eluded everyone, even the seemingly smarter detectives. A similar path can be taken for solving the issues of a stuck career. Start by asking simple questions that are so simple they almost seem dumb. Questions like,"Where am I?" Sounds like a common sense question, right? No. The answer to that question is a lot more complex than "I am the Director of Operations for a Fortune 500 company." This answer should also explore how far away from the goal are you, do you have the education you need to go to your desired goal, are you financially able to support your own growth and development... Ask the dumb questions because sometimes those simple question produce answers that are the key to discovering why you are currently stuck and how you may get unstuck.

The fourth step to getting unstuck is to develop a strategy. In the 1950, Dr. Alice Stewart discovered there was a link between a woman getting her abdomen x-rayed during pregnancy and increased rates of childhood cancer. Those children born to women who had their abdomens x-rayed during pregnancy had higher rates of childhood cancer. Dr. Stewart conducted her research and presented her information to the academy. However, it was not until the 1970's that the practice of x-raying a woman's abdomen during pregnancy was stopped. For 20 years the academy had the information needed to lower the rates of childhood cancer but did nothing. The information was there but it had no impact on childhood cancer rates. Why? Because information is inanimate. Information is meant for use and application. Failure to use the information makes the information useless. The same is true for your career.

In step three you asked yourself the "why" questions. After you answer the question and have the information, the next step is to use that information to develop a strategy. The strategy is to take the answers to your question and identify solutions. If your answer is "I do not have the education I need to get to the the position I want", the strategy needs to include how to achieve what you need to eliminate that problem, go to school. Strategies are action packed and time sensitive. "I am going to go back to school" is not a strategy. "By August of this year I will complete and submit my college application to be considered for early admissions, I will get accepted and begin work on my Masters of Divinity in August of next year. I will take 12 hours per semester to complete my degree in two years and ..." is a strategy. There are three elements to a good strategy:

1. Problem Identification: what is the reason a strategy needs to be developed. Refer back to step number 3 of getting unstuck.
2. Problem Solution: clear and concise action steps to solve the problem. Action steps mean that there needs to be something that has to be done beyond thinking about it. There should be movement, writing, networking, negotiating, researching, and action.
3. Timeline: year, month and the possible day the action step will be accomplished.

Strategy steps should be SMART (Specific, Measurable, Attainable, Realistic and Time Sensitive)

The fifth step to getting unstuck is the implementation of the strategy. A strategy that is never implemented is just as bad as good information that is never used. After documenting the strategy there must be the implementation of the strategy. This simply means that you do what the strategy says. The strategy is a road map to your destination, the implementation is you following the navigation. It is a conscious decision to take responsibility for your career by taking expressed action to change what has gone wrong, make it right and move forward.

The sixth step is to assess and adjust. Even the best plans require adjustments from time to time. The path to career goal achievement is not about making one path work it is about developing a path that works for you. Life happens to everyone and no living person is exempt. The best plans can be altered by illness, happy family addition, company downsizing and the list could go on. Even if none of those life altering things happen, plans can still need adjustment. Along the way a person may discover a change in their passions or that they no longer want to advance in the career they initially thought.

In this instance it does not make sense to stay on a path that no longer leads to where you want to go: assess where you are and readjust your plan. Make adjustments based on what is not working and then alter the direction of your journey.

To get unstuck you have six easy steps to remember:

1. Acknowledge that you are stuck
2. Take responsibility for your role in being stuck and for getting yourself unstuck
3. Look for the "why" of how you got stuck
4. Develop a strategy based on the answers to your "why" questions
5. Implement the strategy
6. Assess and readjust

You now have your steps to getting unstuck so, it seems that would be the end, but it is not. Now you must take these steps and plan your escape from the middle. Before you can plan your escape you must take an assessment of all the things you have at your disposal. Things that will help you achieve the desired goal, an assessment of you because you are the major "results changing" factor in the equation that equals your career goal achievement. It is important that you take a full inventory of your ability to impact your career. Be clear about what you know (knowledge), who you know (network), what you have done (skills) and what you can do (abilities).

Secondly, you must be willing to accept the truth about

yourself. Confucius says "He Who Knows Not And Knows Not That He Knows Not Is A Fool - Shun Him." The person that is unaware of themselves will do foolish things, create foolish expectations and take a foolish approach to their career. Such an approach can be worse than career limiting, it can be career ending. To be successful you must asses yourself and be honest about what you find. If the assessment is done correctly and thoroughly,you will discover things that may not be pleasing to you. This is not the time to deny that you have flaws, this is the time to be honest with yourself and to give others permission to tell you the truth. This is not a step for the faint of heart. In this time you may learn things that hurt your feelings and make you feel resentful towards those who have withheld this information. A common question professionals ask during this period is "Why didn't you tell me?" The key to this step is to ask questions that produce an actionable response. Before you ask the question think to yourself "will the answer to this question result in an action item?" If the answer will result in an action item, then, you are asking the right question. This method keeps you forward focused. It is difficult, but, fight the inclination to focus on the "I should have..." and focus on the "I am going to..." "I should have" questions makes you focus your energy on things you have no control over, things you cannot impact, things that are a waist of your time. While, "I am going to"-statements allow you to focus your energy on action steps, things that are in your control to do and change.

Research

Once you have acknowledged your situation of being stuck, you have decided to get unstuck and your destination has been determined, research must begin. Research is vital to getting unstuck. In our society we research everything: parents do extensive research on day care facilities and schools, potential car buyers research vehicle choices, employees research employers and vice versa. With the worldwide web at our fingertips, research is now easier than ever. If we research everything else, why not our careers and the paths we should take to achieve success in our career. This research includes research on the intended career, The traditional paths people take to success in the career, people who have been successful in the selected career and the paths they took to their success. This phase is where you begin to identify the path you need to take to reach your career destination. Your research should reveal what types of companies hire your desired career, it should also reveal the minimum qualifications as well as the preferred qualifications. Research should also reveal who the "industry leaders" happen to be.

Let's pause for a second to define a few terms: minimum qualifications, preferred qualifications and industry leader. Every career has these three things and if you are to begin work, be successful or be the best in your desired career you must know, understand and achieve these three things. First, let's understand, companies desire to hire people that will be successful; job descriptions, hiring practices, interviews, performance evaluations and the entire employment process from beginning to end is designed with the success of the employee in mind.

- Minimum qualifications: these are the minimum requirements to be considered for the job. This may be as low as two years of high school or as high as a PhD. The important things to note is that the minimum qualification or the minimum hiring standard (MHS) is a barrier to entry not a key to success. Organizations are typically not looking to hire, retain or promote a person who is minimally qualified for the job. Most companies and hiring managers are looking for a person at the top of the talent pool and will often hire and promote based on the preferred qualifications. You must attain the minimum, but, the minimum is not your goal.

- Preferred qualifications: often called the "preferreds", these are the qualifications companies really want a person to have when they fill a position. Many professionals get confused by the preferred qualifications and think the idea behind them is simply to have a check list. This thinking is a fallacy and may result in a missed opportunity. The preferred qualifications are about success factors. For example: a posted position may have a minimum qualification of a Bachelors degree and a preferred qualification of a Masters of Business Administration (MBA). Does this mean the company is only looking for a person with a MBA? No! The company has identified, from experience, from other companies, job requirements, that those with MBAs demonstrate a higher level of understanding and ability to do the job well. Both understanding and ability lead to success. Companies want to hire people that will be successful because successful employees make companies money.

- Industry leader: these are the go to people for a particular topic. This could be within an industry and may even be specific to a company. A person can be the industry leader within a company. This means when there is a question on a topic most everyone looks to this person, not because of their title, but because of their expertise in the area. They typically have the right answers or are savvy at walking people through a process that leads to resolution. These people are the problem solvers for their area of expertise.

Research about your desired career path must lead you to the minimum qualifications, preferred qualifications and the industry leader, if the research is done correctly. This information is vital because it helps you understand the education, years of experience and KSA's (Knowledge, Skills and Abilities) needed to perform the job. This is the first step to developing your path of achievement. While all these things are important to find out it is also critical that your research reveal potential mentors.

A good mentor is not someone who makes you "feel good." A good mentor's role is to ask the hard questions, make the uncomfortable observation and push you to your point of success. A good mentor says what needs to be said in order to get the desired results. The surprise may be that a good mentor does not have to be in your desired industry or career choice. Sometimes, the best mentors are those that may be supported by your desired career. For example, if you desire to be the COO (Chief Operating Officer) it is likely a good idea to have a CEO (Chief Executive Officer) for a mentor. Why? Typically the CEO is one of the decision makers on a COO search. The CEO can tell you the exact skills decision makers are looking for when selecting a COO.

A good mentor can be the difference between a stumbling block and a road block. A good mentor makes their hindsight your foresight: this means the mentor has a philosophy that you do not have to make the same mistakes they made. This allows you to start ahead of the game: you will make mistakes but, if you follow your mentors advice and guidance, you will not have to make the same mistakes they made. The key to a good mentor is they warn you about potential potholes in the road and help you navigate around the roadblocks and minefields on your road to success. They have made mistakes that you can learn from and they are not afraid to tell you. A good mentor can be instrumental in assessing and telling you what is in your way.

If you are going to get unstuck you will have to do your research, learn about successful people in your desired career and get a top notch mentor who will compassionately but honestly guide you through the process.

Chapter Five

There is one quality more important than "know-how." This is "know-what" by which we determine not only how to accomplish our purposes, but what our purposes are to be.
~Norbert Wiener

Redefining the "top"

The phrase "the top" has become cliche; everyone says they want to be there and we are all trying to find our place at the top. But what is the top and is there one universal top or is my top different than yours? Another reason many professionals are stuck is because they have no clue what the top is. Let's get more specific: they don't know where the top is for them.

Stuck professionals struggle to get unstuck because they are not passionate about where they would go if they moved from their current positions: they have no passion for their work, their industry, their path. Imagine working everyday as a veterinarian when you don't like animals or working as a pilot when you are afraid of flying or being a daycare worker when you don't really like children. Why would one do this? Peer pressure, parent pressure, societal pressure may answer this question. Schools today try to do a great job of exposing children to the many career options but still fall short. Growing up I heard nothing of Human Resources as a profession, not even in college. I knew that successful people were doctors or lawyers and I wanted to be successful, so, I decided on a doctor. I went to college to be a doctor, a neurosurgeon to be specific. Knowing the person I am today, I would have been miserable as a doctor. This is true for many professionals who find themselves stuck. They have selected a career path using faulty data and now they are stuck.

I once had a client who was very bright, went to the best schools, was a rising star in a huge firm and was on her way to what everyone else deemed "the top." She was rising and rising fast until all of a sudden she found herself stuck, but could not understand why. The problem was the top in her journey was a place of misery for her. Her passion did not lie at the "top" of that company. It actually lied in a non-profit organization where she could impact lives differently. She was subconsciously sabotaging her own career because she was heading to top she defined as her "personal hell." Not an ideal way to spend a career.

The question is not "what is the top?" the question is "what is your top?" When asked the question differently many people have to stop and redefine "the top." The top is relative to what drives you, what makes you tick, what you find fulfilling and it must be defined by you. The top is the top you choose. The top does have a few characteristics. The major characteristic is it makes you happy, you actually enjoy it. It is important that you do not confuse enjoy with easy. The top is far from easy, often it is the hardest work you will ever do, but, you will find that you enjoy the work, it brings you pleasure.

Make a Plan and Make it Plain

A lot of work has happened up to this point. You have:

- Assessed your career
- Accepted the things about yourself that have contributed to your stuck situation
- Determined a career destination
- Identified your definition of the top

- Reviewed how you were able to achieve your current success including your failures
- Determined what actions, activities, people and places have presented obstacles
- Researched your desired destination, possible paths, qualifications and potential mentors; and
- Now you are ready to develop a strategic plan to move forward.

Strategic planning is an overused term. People often use the term "strategic" before a word when they want to make what they are doing sound important or grander than it is. Strategic is not just a puff up word, it is word that actually impacts the definition. A strategic plan is not just some words for people to say or a goa;l that people like to aim toward. The strategic plan is something that people do, they live it and achieve their goal(s) through the very objective and clear action items and timelines included in the plan. It is more than a sexy title, it is a roadmap to your desired career achievement.

The strategic career plan is so objective and detailed that it can be placed on a spread sheet. Follow the recommendation of Stephen Covey and "Start with the end in mind." Think of your retirement party: there will be huge gathering of people, there will be food, fun, gifts, a live band, the president of the United States will be there and fun will be had by all. Perhaps that is overkill, but you get the point. On that day you will be celebrated for being the best...? Think to that day, think of the title you will be called and write that title on your spreadsheet. The next step is to begin to work backwards, what is the position before your retirement position? Write that position on the line above your retirement title, and continue that process, working backwards to your current position. Now, you have the framework for your plan, a skeleton.

The next step is to add meat to the bones of your plan. Take a look at the job you consider to be your next career step. This should be the next line on your spreadsheet. This will be the first position you begin to research extensively. You want to find out what it takes to be the most qualified person for this positions; the education, years of experience, certifications, professional organization memberships, etc. Each requirement should get its own box or line so that you are able to track when you have achieved that particular requirement. Begin to fill in your spreadsheet with the items you have identified. The spreadsheet should be comprehensive, remember you are not trying to be a good candidate, you are trying to be the best candidate. The spreadsheet, once completed should be used as a plan to follow. You should go about your career making every effort to check things off the spreadsheet.

How does the spreadsheet work? The spreadsheet is your checklist: these are things you are working to accomplish in preparation for your next positions/the next step in your career. For example: if the next step in your career is to become a CPA you know you will need a degree in accounting, and, to take and pass the CPA exam. Each of these would be three different steps on your spreadsheet. Once you achieve each step, you would check it off on the spreadsheet. Some steps will happen simultaneously, while others, will require another step be completed before it can be achieved. As your spreadsheet begins to fill up with checks you know you are ready and qualified for your "next step" position. Your spreadsheet is the plan you will follow to get to your career goal, that fun filled retirement party. In that appendix is an example of what the strategic career plan spreadsheet looks like, as well as an empty sheet for you to begin using.

Failure has to be an option
I was afraid to fall and then I fell and falling lost its power.
~Lux Atl

The fear of heights is an interesting fear. Though it is identified as a fear of heights it is not. People are not afraid of being up high; what would being up high do? Though the fear manifests itself when the person is at a high altitude, what they are actually afraid of is the high altitude turning into a low altitude at an extremely rapid pace, which would result in them being a spot on the pavement: they actually have a fear of falling. The fear of heights is often so deeply rooted that the person paralyzed by the fear does not even remember where or when the fear began, they just know they cannot experience life the way those around them experience it and they miss out because of their fear of falling. The same is true for professionals, especially those who are stuck. Risks are a part of life and so is failure. Sometimes, even the best plans fail, but those who have planned and are focused on achieving their goals, have a better chance of rebounding and getting back on track quickly. When I think of success through failure I think of Michael Jordan who said "I've missed more than 9000 shots in my career. I've lost almost 300 games. 26 times, I've been trusted to take the game winning shot and missed. I've failed over and over and over again in my life. And that is why I succeed." Michael Jordan is arguably one of the best basketball players of all times, not known at all for his failures. Why is he not known for his 9000 missed shots, after all 9000 is a lot of times to miss, especially when you are paid tens of millions of dollars to make the shot? His failures were just practice shots for the shots that mattered, the overwhelming successes that resulted from his practice and his willingness to take a risk, fail and rebound.

Revise the plan

Life happens and plans change which is why career plans are made for revision. A great professor once said "There is no writing just rewriting." The same is true for your career plan. Your career plan must always be in a state of revision and updating based on your professional environment and your place in life. Don't be afraid to change directions or career paths. Life may put things on hold or speed certain achievements up, you may even get recognized and skip a few steps in your career. When life happens take a little time to refocus and document the new direction. Don't get sidetracked or lose focus; documenting the revisions helps.

Be held accountable

Weight watchers is a highly successful weight loss program. There are many things that lend to its success. It is no secret that proper diet is a key to weight loss and weight watchers has designed a system that allows people to understand their food intake better. Though that is helpful and surely a component of the success of the program, the thing that can be given the most credit is the accountability portion of the program. Many weight watchers groups meet once a week. At that weekly meeting people discuss different topics, their struggles, recipes, success, but most importantly, the meeting leader shows up with a weight watcher digital scale and weighs everyone. In the meeting you will see people all but stripping down to their undergarments; they remove coats, shirts, belts, shoes, socks, most anything they can take off without being inappropriate. Why? Because they know that someone will look at their weight loss and be able to tell if they have kept their commitment, if they did what they said they would do: they will be held accountable. There is something about knowing that you have to go before a group, get on a scale, look someone in the face and have to explain why you did or did not achieve the intended goal-to lose weight. The same is true for your career plan. You may have the fortitude to achieve your career goals on your own but having an accountability partner is a must. You need someone who you must report to concerning your progress. This person should be someone you trust and someone who you allow to be honest with you. They should get a copy of your plan and at least one hour of your time to have you explain the plan in detail to them. After they understand your plan the accountability begins. They must hold you accountable for doing what you have said you will do in the time that you have designated. They will ensure you either complete your assignments or change the plan as necessary.

Chapter Six

The shortest distance between two points assumes you know where you're going.
~Robert Brault

Start the journey

You have assessed, researched, defined the top, made a plan and found an accountability partner. Now it is time to move. The best plan in the world is useless if you do not get moving. It is important to have a great plan to follow but it must be followed and action has to be taken. In order to succeed you have to get off the couch and take the first step.

Keep moving

A mountain stands between you and the thing you need to survive. Do you A: start digging to get to the other side of the mountain or B: walk around the mountain? The answer is, it depends. It depends on what will be the quickest route. Drilling through a mountain is no easy task, especially when walking around is probably more practical. The same is true in your career. Many people are stuck because they are trying to take the "shortest" route instead of the route that makes the most sense for them. The shortest distance between two points is a straight line but that may not be the fastest way to the finish line. You will have to blaze your own path but don't drill a path through the mountain if you don't have to.

The other thing you must be prepared for are obstacles and unforeseen happenings. Both are a part of life and will be a part of your career. Plan for them. Having a plan B, C and

D or a "what if" plan is essential. You have to have a plan to keep moving toward your goal no matter what obstacles may happen. Some obstacles may render you motionless for a time but having a "bounce back" plan makes recovery easier.

Chapter Seven

If you are irreplaceable you are unpromotable.
~Dethra U. Giles

The worst enemy anyone can ever have is the enemy disguised as a friend. Many professionals have a very real enemy, one that is killing them emotionally, physically and in their career. This "friend" has them stressed out and has limited their ability to move up in their current company. Even when they leave their current company the professional often takes express care to take this "friend" with them and maintain an intimate relationship. This "friend" goes by the name of "Irreplaceable." Professionals often pride themselves on being irreplaceable: the person a company, department, division or supervisor cannot live without.

This book would not be complete if the issue of being irreplaceable was not addressed. There are two concerns to address here:

1. The idea of being irreplaceable in a company, organization, department, etc. is a myth; and
2. You never want to be irreplaceable

The myth

There is nothing new under the sun." It is difficult to trace who first said this phrase but it is often quoted and is very true. Most of us do not have knowledge that cannot be attained by others or does not exist elsewhere in a place where another person can learn and master the information. If you were to get hit by the proverbial bus, the company where you work would likely not stop functioning, would not go bankrupt and would not close its doors. Things might slow down for a day, week, maybe even a month, they may even close for a day so your co-workers could visit you in the Intensive Care Unit. When a company or supervisor says you are "irreplaceable" what they really mean is "we cannot pay someone what we pay you and still get the work done. We really like the work you do and it benefits us tremendously to have you in that role. Please stay forever." It may even mean "we would have to pay three people to do what you do." It feels good to be wanted, needed even, and human natures soaks up this feeling. Because of the pride associated with the designation, professionals wear the brand of "irreplaceable" like a proud NFL player wearing a Super Bowl championship ring and they believe it. Many professionals will begin to believe they are irreplaceable. Here is the hard truth: no matter what a supervisor says, there is a 99.9% chance that you are, indeed, irreplaceable. This is not meant to crush your ego or to minimize your value to your organization but it is intended to give you a reality check so you may change your perspective on how you operate.

Don't be irreplaceable

Professionals are not the only ones that believe they are irreplaceable. Management even buys into the idea that a person cannot be replaced and this is when the "friend" becomes an enemy. If company leadership believes you cannot be replaced then they also fear the idea of promoting you. I remember working with a client who was stuck in her career. She could not figure out why she made more money than her boss and any time she complained, the company would give her more money, but every time the higher level position opened up she would not get the job. Her question was "If they love me so much, whey won't they give me the job?" They did love her, she was the best person they had in that department, she was the only person that knew the system and she wanted it that way. She wanted to be irreplaceable, she wanted the company dependent on her so she could ensure that she had "job security." She got her wish, but, her wish got her stuck. To promote her meant taking her away from the very reason they valued her existence in the company and why would they do that. She could not be promoted because promoting her meant the company had to replace her and she was irreplaceable. When she worked with me she discovered this was a pattern for her. She would leave one company because she found herself stuck, she would get to the next company and repeat the same career limiting behaviors that got her stuck and labeled as irreplaceable in the previous company. Before she could get unstuck she had to change the pattern of making herself irreplaceable. Once she accepted that being irreplaceable was career limiting and changed the behavior that got her the label, she found herself advancing quickly. Being irreplaceable is not what you want to be, it is not your friend and the only thing it secures is that you will be stuck in your career.

Frequently Asked Questions

1. **I am great at my job, actually the best so why am I stuck in this position?**

    Our grandparents only told us part of the truth, in many instances, they told us the only part they knew. We were told "Go to work, do your job, do it well, stay out of trouble and you will go far, you will make it to the top of your company." While that is partially true, your career is not always based on how good you are at your job. You cannot neglect doing your job and doing it well, it is a major component, you must be good at your job to move up. However, just being good at your job is not enough anymore. Many people, especially middle managers, neglect the importance of the "people" aspect of their position. They keep their nose to the grindstone and do their "job" better than anyone else but totally lose focus on what their "real" job is.

    When you are hired as an entry level professional you are hired to learn and do the technical pieces of the job: you are paid for your technical skills. Bean counters are hired to count beans. As you advanced in your career you begin to be paid for your people skills. The higher you move, the more you are paid for your people skills. Think of the CEO, she spends most of her career in meetings, doing very little technical work. The CEO's job is the deal with people, make sure the workforce has what it needs to achieve the mission, make sure the stockholders are happy, make sure the vision is cast for the company. The CEO of the bean counting company does not count beans. If you want to move up you have to grasp the "people" side of things. The "people" side is the biggest obstacle for many middle managers. This happens because no one ever communicates the need to switch gears. Entry level people are promoted and given bonus for being good at the technical piece. The behavior is rewarded. There are all types of studies that show the best method for getting a person to repeat a particular behavior is to reward that behavior. As a result the reward of promotion or bonus encourages people to repeat the behavior that got them the reward, doing their technical job well. As they continue to get promoted they continue to focus on the technical piece, they become more and more technically proficient while complaints of poor people management are continuously lodge against them with Human Resources. Because it becomes evident to decision makers that this person cannot manage people, projects or tasks, at a certain point they stop getting promoted. Why? Because they have been promoted to their level of incompetence. They have not taken the time to learn people because no one ever told them they needed to do so. No one communicated that they were being promoted not to become more technically savvy but for them to make a team of people as savvy as they were. They missed the importance of stepping from behind the desk and talking to the people.

2. **Everyone that gets promoted around here just kisses butt and I just can't do that. What else can I do to get promoted?**

Pucker up! Just kidding. Honestly, this commonly stated but rarely defined term must be defined. What is "kissing but?" I have worked with many coaching clients who complain that "People who get promoted are all kissing butt." When asked to define "kissing butt", they define basic networking and career improvement activities. I had one client to say "They do stuff like say 'good morning' to everyone. Or, go over and shake people's hands at events." Volunteering to do extra work, going to lunch, participating in after-hours company functions like the Christmas party, golf tournaments, fund raisers etc. Going the extra mile to get noticed is not "kissing butt" it is called "getting promoted." If those things are not "kissing butt" then what is? Kissing but is what people do when there is no relation to the job. For example: your boss is extremely over weight and has not lost a pound in six years, yet you have co-worker that insists on flattering the boss by asking "Have you lost weigh?" The boss sucks it up and the employee knows it. That is kissing butt, the compliments have nothing to do with the job, with enhancing job skill or with demonstrating an ability to do a higher level job. The opposite is attending an after hours event. This demonstrates an ability to meet and network with new clients which demonstrates an acumen for building new relationship, fostering current relationships which all relates to client relations. It is very important to know the difference because it can be the difference between staying stuck and getting unstuck.

3. **I am not willing to go to company picnics, Christmas parties, golf tournaments, etc. I just want to do my job and do it well. What is wrong with that?**

Nothing is wrong with wanting to go to work, do your job well and go home. The problem is, most people who make this statement don't really mean it. What they actually mean is, "I want to do my job, do it well AND get promoted without doing all that other stuff."

The get promoted part is where the trouble lies. I wish I had better news for you and could tell you the other "stuff" was not required, but I can't. If I did, I would be a liar and a worthless Executive Coach. The truth is, to advance in your career you have to grasp the people side of things. Being able to effectively deal with, manage and network with people becomes increasingly important as you move up in your career. Perhaps you think this is not true. Show me a CEO that does not see more people than he sees paper. Leaders are notoriously in meetings all day, which is why they have to pay close attention to their work/life balance; not because they have so much work but because most of their work day is spent in meetings doing the people stuff so they spend their non-working day doing the paper stuff. The people matter and failing to do the people stuff may result in a slow progression to the place you want to be.

4. **I hear what you have been saying and the truth is I don't know what I want to be when I grow up. How do I find that out?**

You are not alone. Many people are confused about where their path should lead them. The first step is acknowledging that you don't know, then commit to finding out. Many are on a path that someone else, or their environment designated for them. Growing up I knew nothing of Human Resources, Executive Coaches, Tenured professors, CPA, CEO, etc. All I knew was success was a doctor or a lawyer. So, I went to college to be a doctor. Had I followed that path, I would have been on a path of misery for me and I would have been stuck. In a moment of honesty I have to admit giving up the "dream" of being a doctor was an emotional journey for me. But, it was a journey that needed to happen. This step can be difficult, emotional and can cause minor debates amongst family members, particularly when the decision has a financial impact on the family. Another method is to go back and look at all the jobs you have held, volunteer work included. Look at the jobs and see what duties you enjoyed the most. Even if you had a job you hated there was at least one aspect of the job that appealed to you. Identify those high points in each job and document them. You will likely begin to notice a theme. This theme will direct you to the type of work you love and want to do.

5. **I know people who have made it and did not do all of this. Why are the rules different for me?**

There are two very different but true answers to this question.

1. The phrase "I know someone who..." is like nails on a chalkboard to many coaches or anyone in the business of helping people. Why? Because, in most instances the statement is not entirely true. "I know someone who..." is code for "I know someone who told me they knew someone's cousin's girlfriend who had a friend who..." The person, "who," is actually a mythical creature, kind of like the loch ness monster: the "who" may really exist but no one has ever really seen them and the people who actually have seen "who" cannot really verify if things were exactly as they seemed. For example, think of yourself. Do you have a high school diploma? If you do, how many people at your job can actually verify that you do. For all practical purposes they could tell anyone that you do not have a high school diploma and you got your

job anyway. That falsehood could spread and then you would be the person "who" got the job without a high school diploma. See, how easy that is. The reality is that no one really knows the intricacies of the career path of "who." The people making the assumption only know what they see. The mythical person "who" really may have done some of the things described in the book, but since no one knows who this mythical person really is, no one can verify or deny the facts about what "who" actually did or did not do to advance their career.

2. There is always an exception to the rule. That exception is not the norm and cannot be consistently used and relied on as a way predict outcomes. One example of an exception is the all time great Spudd Webb. Spudd Webb was about 5'7" when he played in the NBA and won the slam dunk championship in February of 1986. The average height for an African American male is 5'10", so at 5'7" Webb was three inches below the average height for an African American male. The average height for a NBA player peaked in 1986, the year Webb won the slam dunk contest. The average height of a NBA player in 1986 was 6'7.62", which made Webb over a foot shorter than the average NBA player. A 5'7" NBA all star is almost unheard of. Webb is the exception: that one person who did not necessarily follow the rules of the game but made it anyway or is he? Webb is a great example of "who." Spud Webb made a huge impact on professional basketball but there was and is no influx of 5 footers in the NBA. If being six feet is required to be in the NBA, Web is the "who" that was not six feet and made it anyway. But, Webb had everything else required: natural skill, speed, leap height, tenacity, work ethic and the list can keep going. The same is true for what it takes

to be a success in your career. There is no one magic bullet to success, it takes a variety of factors coming together to make it happen: just like being six feet tall, alone, does not make a person a basketball player, being just good at your job, or just networking, or just going to school won't get you to the top. Success takes all of those factors coming together. Let's say that one of the preferred qualifications for being the director of a department is to have a college degree and most all the other directors have a college degree but one of the directors only has a high school diploma. There is a 99.9% chance that this person is stellar and exceeds the requirements in all the other areas of the job. There will always be a rare few who defy the normal path to success and succeeded anyway but those people are few and far between and should not be used as the standard for how one should develop a path to success. I am not saying that you are not the person to defy the standard for what works, there is no reason you can't be. I am saying that the odds are not in your favor.

Case Studies

These case studies are taken from real life coaching clients. The names have been changed but the scenarios are real.

John

John has been recently promoted to supervisor. He is very excited and so is everyone around him. All of his peers feel there is no one more deserving than John. The leadership of the region feel the same way. John has worked very hard to get to where he is and plans to continue the same route he has been on: working hard, doing his job well and being the best. Those three things have been the keys John's success to this point.

What should John do?

John is at a pivotal point; he is at the proverbial "fork in the road" of his career. This juncture is the point where many middle managers make the wrong decision. The first thing John needs to do is an assessment. John needs to assess where he would like to go, where he is and what it will take to bridge the two. Many people miss this step and find themselves stuck. They never do an assessment. Following John's assessment he needs to develop a strategic plan for his career. This plan should clearly identify the Knowledge, Skills and Abilities (KSA's) needed to reach the next and ultimate levels of his career.

Aside from identifying the necessary KSA's John needs to also identify the necessary "people" aspects of his career advancement. An important part of John's strategic plan needs to be building his network. This may mean learning golf or tennis, increasing his social networking presence and attending more networking events. Lastly, and probably most importantly, John has to realize that what got him to where he is will likely not get him to where he is going and be willing to make the necessary adjustments to his plan. The bottom line is John has to carefully map out his career and develop a path to get to where he plans to go.

Keisha

Keisha is the best accountant around. She is young and rose to management pretty quickly. When she first arrived at the firm the Regional Manager told her "You will run this region one day" and Keisha believed him. Now, Keisha is beginning to doubt the Regional Manger's words. She has been an Accounting Supervisor for five years and has not even heard a whisper about her being promoted, though at least four positions have opened and been filled. Keisha consistently gets high ratings on her evaluations. 90% of her areas are rated "exceeds expectations" except one. The area of "Interpersonal skills" is always her lowest area. It is never unacceptable but is never high. She ignores the poor rating and does not address it with a clear action plan. She decided it is not that important particularly because no one can ever clearly explain how she can improve in this area or even what this area actually is. She has only heard one side comment from a previous supervisor who said "You can be difficult to work with sometimes." When Keisha snapped back and said "What is that supposed to mean" he quickly clammed up and dropped the conversation.

What should Keisha do?

Keisha, like John needs to do an assessment. Many middle managers miss the "themes" of their career. Themes are not good or bad; they are neutral. Human nature is to pay attention and cling to those themes that are good. You will find people who are able to spout verbatim career highlights, the things they are told they do well, but not so much for those areas of improvement.

One theme for Keisha has been the need to improve her interpersonal skills. This needs to be a focal point if Keisha wants to leave the middle. Executive level career advancement is directly correlated to people skills. When a person enters the workforce they are hired for what they know, when they are promoted in the workforce it is because of who they know. Is this to imply that knowing the job is completely irrelevant? Absolutely not.

Knowing the job is critical but everyone in the middle knows the job; what distinguishes one middle manager from another are the people skills. Look at the big consulting firms and examine what the partners in those firms do. They don't do accounting, organizational development, training or finance, they do the people piece. They are not paid for their technical knowledge they are paid for their ability to work with and influence people. Leaders know this is important and they look for this skill when they are considering which middle managers to promote. If Keisha is to move up in the organization she has to pay attention and fine tune this skill.

Ishan

Ishan is a young professional with tons of potential. He is anxious to do a great job, has tons of ideas and is always picked to serve on projects but he is getting very frustrated. When he joined the firm he was promoted three times in two years. Now he has been in the same management position for three years and thinks he should have been promoted by now. He is thinking of leaving the firm because he does not feel they recognize his potential.

What should Ishan do?

Ishan's situation is more common today than ever. There are Ishan's all over the place. Like John and Keisha, Ishan needs to do an assessment. All assessments should end with a plan, a realistic plan. In Ishan's assessment he needs to determine the realistic timeline for the advancement he would like to achieve.

Ishan is making a very common mistake: not being realistic about the time it takes to master a skill. Many people want to move and they want to move up the ladder quickly. In some instances this happens but in most instances "slow and steady wins the race." I worked with a very bright woman who was the CEO of a successful company and she use to say "People are promoted to their level of incompetence and then are left there." This is the case many times when people are promoted too quickly; and would be the case if Ishan achieved the success he desired in the time he wanted. When a person is promoted too quickly they often miss the opportunity to master the skills offered by the prior position. When a person misses key and fundamental skills they often don't realize they missed these key skills until it is too late. One good example is sports, martial arts in particular. Advancement in martial arts is predicated on the student learning and mastering the moves of the current belt. Why? Senseis understand that later, more complex moves are based on the foundation of the moves learned at the beginner, white belt, no stripes level. The person who does not master the guard stance is not able to do a spinning crescent kick or any combination that includes a transition to or from a guard stance. The same is true for a career; each level of a career has something that must be mastered in order to be successful at the next level and subsequent levels. Leaving one level too quickly could mean leaving the opportunity to master those much needed lesson of that level.

Ishan should assess the actual amount of time it takes to master the skill(s) he needs to learn from his current position. The higher the position, the longer time a person must spend mastering the skills. Once he has assessed the true amount of time he should spend, then he can better determine whether he is being passed over for promotions or if he is being allowed to master an important skill that will be needed at a later date.

Conclusion

Don't waste time learning the "tricks of the trade." Instead, learn the trade.
~Attributed to both James Charlton and H. Jackson Brown, Jr.

I wish I had better news and could tell you there was a quick shortcut to the top but if there is one I don't have it. What I can offer are simple, practical, tried and true tools that work. No shortcuts, no tricks, just real work that produces results. Life presents obstacles but the biggest, most consistent obstacle we have is us. We are typically in our own way. If you are truly going to be successful you must first discover how you get in your own way and make a conscious decision to stop doing those thing. Stop getting in your own way. Once you are determined to stop getting in the way of achieving your career goals then follow the steps outlined:

- Assess where you are and how you got there
- Identify where you are going and a plan to get there
- Revise your plan when needed
- Be held accountable by yourself and others
- Take action to begin your journey; and
- Keep moving

These steps will get you on your path to success and will help you get "Unstuck."

Articles

This Job is In Your Way
~Dethra U. Giles

The Batman Career Philosophy
~Dethra U. Giles

This Job is In Your Way

Tasha Johnson went to college with high hopes. She had dreams of being the CFO of a Fortune 500 Company, being seen as the leading authority on Finance and being one of the "financial experts" interviewed for commentary on the nation's debt. Tasha, for as long as she could remember, had visualized her first real job: she would be fresh out of college, new degree in hand with two job offers both with a starting salary of $65,000.00 annually and a healthy benefits package to match. So, for the life of her she could not imagine why she was sitting in her fourth interview, six months after graduating at the top of her class getting ready to turn down another "entry level" job that paid too little and wanted too much. Tasha, though a fictitious character, symbolizes what many go thorough at some point in their career: the discouraging point where expectation and reality meet.

Some of the best life quotes and life advice come from movies. The new movie Transformers 3: Dark of the Moon has a scene that speaks to Tasha and many other's career situation. There is a scene where Sam Witwiky, one of the main characters, is very frustrated because of the difficulty he faces finding the job he wants. Witwiky has been instrumental in saving the world twice and has a medal of honor from the President to prove it, however, these credential do not serve him well in his job search. On his last interview, when he is ready to decline the job, the hiring official tried to discourage Witwiky from declining the job and says "The job you want is the one after this one but this job is in the way." The hiring manager went on to tell Witwiky that if he performed well in the job he was being offered the position he wanted, the higher level, better paying, more prestigious position was eminent. This same scenario is lived out in many careers except, unlike Witwiky, there is often no one to communicate that "this job is in the way of the job you want." How different would your job search, work ethic, perspective about your current situation be if you viewed your current job, the job you hate, as the job you had to do and do well before you got the position you wanted.

What is so important about the "Job that is in the way"? The answer is simple: preparation for sustained success. Another movie reference is Karate Kid. Whether you remember the old Karate Kid, Ralph Macchio, or the new Karate Kid, Jaden Smith, you remember that the teacher did not start the student off with a full fight or any real karate moves. The teacher started the student out doing things that seemed completely unrelated to fighting which frustrated the student. Everyone can quote the famous line "Wax on, wax off." It was the elementary, seemingly unrelated moves that developed the Karate kid into the best fighter in town. Sure, the famous crane kick won the fight but it was the "wax on, wax off" that kept the Karate Kid alive long enough to do the famous winning kick. The "wax on, wax off" was what ensured and sustained his success in the fight. In the learning process the teacher would not allow the Karate Kid to move on to become a prize fighter until he mastered the most elementary move. For the Karate Kid "wax on, wax off" was the job that was in the way. The same is true for most careers; the job that is in the way is the "wax on, wax off" of your career. You must master it in order to go to the next spot.

This message resonates with many of you but you think it is talking about someone else. There is a seasoned professional reading this article and thinking "You tell those young folks. Please get them straight about paying their dues. But what about me, I have paid my dues and am tired of being overlooked. Not only have I mastered 'wax on, wax off' I have also taught it to other people and they mastered it and moved on. So this article cannot be for me." You are the exact person this article is for.

Every rung of the career ladder requires a mastery of additional skills. Careers are limited, slowed down or even ended because many professionals, particularly season professionals, don't recognize when to shift skill sets. There are two things that employees are paid for: people skills and technical skills. At the beginning of a career organizations pay for technical skills, the actual job itself. As a career progresses organizations begin to pay more for people skills, managing people, networking, getting contracts, making deals. Let us look at another movie character to make this a trifecta of character references. One of the most amazing and intriguing superheroes of all time is Batman. It has been said that Batman has no real superpower but that could not be further from the truth. Batman has no real physical superpower but Batman has superhuman knowledge. He is a genius and as a result he can create and build gadgets that makes him able to do most things the other superheroes are able to do. This is what puts Batman in the top five of Superheroes. What sets him apart and makes him the most powerful is his knowledge of people. Batman knows his friends as well as his enemies inside and out and has an intricate plan to either promote or destroy them. He has mastered the business of people. Many seasoned professionals are stuck and frustrated because they cannot fathom why their careers are not moving: they are good at their job, have a sought after expertise, get glowing evaluations and phenomenal raises. So why are their careers stagnant? They have not mastered the Batman career philosophy. What is that and how is it implemented?

The Batman career philosophy is...

Tune in next time same bat-time, same bat-station and we will talk about it.

The Batman Career Philosophy

The last time we were together we talked about how to gain career advice from cinema. We talked about Transformers III, the Karate Kid and we ended up with Batman. Batman is one of the top super heroes of all time, however, he has no physical super powers. He cannot fly on his own accord, leap a building in a single bound, stop a bullet and cannot take being shot without eminent death. Batman has the same amount of superhuman power as you and I, none. With the odds stacked against him, Batman is still one of the top superheroes. When we consider that Batman does not possess actual superpowers, a legitimate question may be "What makes Batman so successful in his career?" Batman's success can be attributed to his career philosophy which is too expansive to outline in this short article. For brevity we will go over three of my favorites:

1. Batman picked a career path that resulted from his passion
2. Batman took responsibility for his career success; and
3. Batman knows his friends and foes equally well.

Batman picked a career path that resulted from his passion

At the age of eight years old Batman witnessed the murder of his parents by a person attempting to mug them. That event propelled Batman to success in his career as a crime fighter, not because he was a part of a tragic event but because the event ignited a passion and purpose in him. If you are to follow Batman's path to success you must identify a career that is fueled by your passion and fulfills your purpose.

What is your source of passion? Your source does not have to be a tragic event it can be an overwhelmingly happy event that made you feel complete, or a time when you were a part of something and said "this is where I belong." Batman is successful in his career because he knows his purpose, he is driven by his passion and has made a conscious career choice that kept both in mind.

Batman took responsibility for his career success

Once Batman determined his career choice he took complete responsibility for his path. Too often employees feel it is the responsibility of the company or the manager to advance their career. Before we can move forward with a productive conversation we must clear up one thing. Your company, your manager, and all those employed by your organization are concerned about their bottom line. They are not in the business of advancing your career they are in the business of making widgets or providing a service. There are companies that are highlighted for their social concern and their investment in their employees. Those companies have done the research and have found that this investment in their employees positively impacts their bottom line. Your advancement is your responsibility. If your employer will not pay for continued education courses then you must decide to make an investment in yourself and your career. If you are to have a successful career you must acknowledge that success or failure is your responsibility. Batman also took responsibility for gaining the appropriate knowledge to be the best and applied it. Batman did not sit on the sidelines with his genius, martial arts expertise, super computer and gadgets galore waiting for his chance; he jumped right in. So much so that his first attempt at crime fighting resulted in him getting a severe beating from the very people he was trying to save. The beating did not stop him, he actually learned from his mistakes and kept moving forward. In taking action you must learn and accept that failure is a must. A person who is afraid to fail is afraid to learn and will never achieve true success. You must decide and take action.

Batman knows his friends and foes equally well

There is an old saying that says "Keep your friends close and your enemies even closer." Batman would not concur with this saying. Batman believes you should know everyone equally well because a friend could quickly become a foe given the right circumstances. Batman has a file folder on his closest superhero friends that clearly outlines their powers, how they operate and how to take them down. His file contains information that cannot be found anywhere else. Should you have a file on how to take your friends down? No. We should strive to be loyal and have integrity in our dealings, business and otherwise. However, there is something to be learned from Batman's philosophy. It is important to know people, how they can help, hurt, progress or hinder your career. There is an important phrase I often use that says "Treat everyone like they are your boss because they just might be." I use this phrase because of the Batman philosophy. I have had many random encounters with people who ended up being in a position to push forward my ideas or my career. At every event take the opportunity to learn more about those around you but don't just learn how they can help you. Since Batman knows the weaknesses of all his friends he is better able to assist them in battle. You can have the same philosophy. Learn about those around you so you can determine how you can best help them. Sometimes helping a friend reach their goal is more than enough and can have a better pay off than you reaching your own.

There is a lot to be learned from cinema. So the next time you are at a theater or home watching movies don't just watch for entertainment purposes. Look and see what you can learn about your career and how to advance it.

Appendix

Career Plan Spreadsheet, Blank
Sample Career Plan Spreadsheet, Completed

CAREER PLAN SPREADSHEET to become a HR Director

Job Title	Place a "X" in this box when a particular KSA is etc.)	KSA (Knowledge, Skills and Abilities: degrees, certifications, classes, years of experience, etc.)	Projected Date	Actual	Cost	Place a "X" in this box when a particular need is acquired	Mentors/Executive Coach/Network/Associations needed (People and things needed to assist in goal achievement. This does not include the KSAs)
Current Positions							

CAREER PLAN SPREADSHEET to become a HR Director

Job Title	Place a "X" in this box when a particular KSA is	KSA (Knowledge, Skills and Abilities: degrees, certifications, classes, years of experience, etc.)	Projected Date	Actual Date	Cost	Place a "X" in this box	Mentors/Executive Coach/Network/Associations needed (People and things needed to assist in goal achievement. This does not include the KSAs)
HR Specialist							
HR Manager	X	BA degree				X	HR Manager Mentor
		5 years HR experience			$0		HR Director Mentor
	X	Project management experience				X	Hire an Executive Coach from ExecuPrep

About the Author

Dethra U. Giles is an executive coach and a national trainer on leadership, organizational growth, conflict resolution and career development. She serves as the Director of Consulting Services for ExecuPrep, LLC, a performance management firm focusing on training, coaching and Human Resources consulting. Dethra is a sought after coach, speaker, and facilitator. She is revolutionizing how executives manage and grow their careers. She combines her years of experience, formal education and practical knowledge to help each client customize a strategy to maximize their potential and achieve success. To learn more about Ms. Giles and ExecuPrep you may visit www.execuprep.com or e-mail her directly at dugiles@execuprep.com.

ExecuPrep

ExecuPrep is revolutionizing how small to mid-size businesses grow. Focusing on organizational development and performance management strategies, ExecuPrep has the expertise to take the mystery out of people management and organizational leadership. ExecuPrep helps entrepreneurs and entrepreneurial minded people handle what matters so they can focus on what makes money. This is why they are affectionately known as the Entrepreneurs' Human Resources Firm.

www.execuprep.com	Web address
info@execuprep.com	Email
twitter.com/ExecuPrep	Twitter
facebook.com/ExecuPrep	FaceBook
linkedin.com/company/ExecuPrep	LinkedIn
770-860-8017	Phone